Summary of

Why Liberalism Failed
Patrick Deneen

Conversation Starters

By Paul Adams
Book Habits

Please Note: This is an unofficial Conversation Starters guide. If you have not yet read the original work, you can purchase the original book here.

Copyright © 2018 by BookHabits. All Rights Reserved. First Published in the United States of America 2018

We hope you enjoy this complimentary guide from BookHabits. Our mission is to aid readers and reading groups with quality thought-provoking material to in the discovery and discussions on some of today's favorite books.

Disclaimer / Terms of Use: This guide is unofficial and unauthorized. It is not authorized, approved, licensed, or endorsed by the original book's author or publisher and any of their licensees or affiliates. Product names, logos, brands, and other trademarks featured or referred to within this publication are the property of their respective trademark holders and are not affiliated with BookHabits. The publisher and author make no representations or warranties with respect to the accuracy or completeness of these contents and disclaim all warranties such as warranties of fitness for a particular purpose.
No part of this publication may be reproduced or retransmitted, electronic or mechanical, without the written permission of the publisher.

Bonus Downloads
*Get Free Books with **Any Purchase** of* Conversation Starters!

Every purchase comes with a FREE download!

Add spice to any conversation
Never run out of things to say
Spend time with those you love

Get it Now

or Click Here.

Scan Your Phone

Tips for Using Conversation Starters:

EVERY GOOD BOOK CONTAINS A WORLD FAR DEEPER THAN the surface of its pages. Questions herein are designed to bring us beneath the surface of the page and invite us into the world that lives on. These questions can be used to:

- Foster a deeper understanding of the book
- Promote an atmosphere of discussion for groups
- Assist in the study of the book, either individually or corporately
- Explore unseen realms of the book as never seen before

Table of Contents

Introducing *Why Liberalism Failed* 6
Discussion Questions 14
Introducing the Author 35
Fireside Questions 42
Quiz Questions 53
Quiz Answers 66
Ways to Continue Your Reading 67

Introducing *Why Liberalism Failed*

WHY LIBERALISM FAILED IS A new political book by Patrick Deneen. Although the title suggests that liberalism has failed, that is not entirely true. Deneen writes that liberalism failed, "not because it fell short, but because it was true to itself." The reason that liberalism has failed in societies is because it has been successful.

Deneen relies on the teachings of a few different political philosophers to write Why Liberalism Failed – most notably, John Locke, Sir

Francis Bacon, and John Stuart Mill. Deneen explains that the base of liberalism rests on a number of different assumptions about human existence. The core of liberalism places the focus on individuals and their liberty. Deneen defines liberty within liberalism as the state in which human beings can be free and unrestricted by the laws in a country. Additionally, liberalism is on a continuous cycle where the new generation gets rid of the previous generation's moral restrictions and economic restrictions.

    According to Deneen, conservatives are classic liberals or "first-wave" liberals. In recent years, many conservatives have used these titles to describe themselves, as well. Today, many conservatives are striving for individualism. On the other side of the political divide, progressive liberals today want a government where the state has some level of control over social policy and economics. Deneen explains that conservatives and liberals think they are against each other. However, what they do not realize is that they actually work together to help each other's goals become achieved. Conservatives work to increase freedom and power, and progressive liberals work to get rid of cultural traditions and cultural norms. Deneen says these to supposedly opposing political parties always advance together. He explains that individualism helps the state become more powerful and authoritative. On the other hand, the state helps to push individualism forward.

The problems that are created by liberalism are also addressed by Deneen. He takes a look at how liberalism affects education, technology, and culture. For example, Deneen explains that liberalism has pushed the creation of cell phones, which have only made people more lonely. The institutions created by liberalism have divided people. "Hook-up culture" and the rising number of people who are addicted to their cell phones, in the opinion of Deneen, are a sign that civilization is about to collapse. His argument is that liberalism is causing people to grow further apart from each other and become more autonomous. Even in schools, Deneen believes that students are no longer following the norms of being honest and modest behavior. Instead, they are cheating more and becoming more rebellious.

Deneen makes it clear in Why Liberalism Failed that he is saddened by the fact that God and organized religion play less of a role in modern society. It has been shown that organized religion has, historically, played a large role in civic engagement in the United States. Deneen is concerned that as religion slowly starts to fade away, society and civic engagement will start to fade away, as well.

In the chapter called "The New Aristocracy," Deneen discusses how liberalism has made way for a new form of aristocracy. He explains that liberalism never intended to completely get rid of the aristocracy. Instead, supporters of liberalism set out in the hopes of tearing down the old system of aristocracy in order to create a newer and better aristocracy.

Finally, Deneen reveals his plan for society to gain freedom from liberalism. The first step is that the achievements in society due to liberalism should be acknowledged. The next step is to "outgrow the age of ideology." This means that political ideologies, such as Marxism, should be tossed out for good. The final step for Deneen is the return of society that is based more on family and religion. This would mean small associations of people that are organized within a local government. In Deneen's opinion, if this were to happen, then communities would start to develop their own culture again, which would mean people would live more fulfilling lives. The alienation brought on by liberalism would vanish.

Deneen believes that society and the government are focusing too much on small – in the grand scheme of things – political issues. People do not realize how severe the threat facing them is. For example, people are concerned about corporations, the government controlling everything, and climate change, just to name a few things. People do not realize that the current way society lives is considered to be unnatural. Deneen believes that it will only be a matter of time before nature begins to fight back.

Discussion Questions

"Get Ready to Enter a New World"

Tip: Begin with questions dealing with broader issues to ensure ample time for quality discussions. Read through all discussion questions before engaging.

~~~

question 1

Patrick Deneen explains that liberalism has failed because it has been successful. What does this mean to you?

~~~

~~~

question 2

What were your expectations of Why Liberalism Failed? How did it live up to your expectations?

~~~

~~~

question 3

What opinion did you have on liberalism before reading Why Liberalism Failed? How did your opinion change after reading?

~~~

~~~

question 4

Patrick Deneen is the author of Why Liberalism Failed. How adequate do you think Deneen's research was? How well did he present his research in the book?

~~~

~~~

question 5

Why Liberalism Failed is a book on liberalism by Patrick Deneen. What was the most interesting section for you to read and why?

~~~

~~~

question 6

In Why Liberalism Failed, Deneen talks about the fading away of organized religion in society being a sign that society will also fade away. What are your thoughts on this?

~~~

~~~

question 7

Patrick Deneen's Why Liberalism Failed is about how liberalism became so successful that it failed humans. What impact did Why Liberalism Failed have on you?

~~~

~~~

question 8

In Why Liberalism Failed, Patrick Deneen makes the claim that even schools are becoming less moral. How accurate do you think this statement is? What are your thoughts on this?

~~~

~~~

question 9

Patrick Deneen speaks out in opposition to what he calls the "hookup culture." What effect do you think "hookup culture" has on society? How new do you think this concept is?

~~~

~~~

question 10

Cell phones and other technology are another aspect of modern society that Deneen uses as an example that society is about to collapse. How has technology affected society, in your opinion? In what ways do you agree and/or disagree with Deneen's position on technology?

~~~

~~~

question 11

Patrick Deneen explains in Why Liberalism Failed that conservatives and progressive liberals actually help each other out and are not as opposite as they believe. What are your thoughts on this concept?

~~~

~~~

question 12

Patrick Deneen defines liberty as the state in which human beings are free and unrestricted by the government. How do you define liberalism?

~~~

~~~

question 13

In the opinion of Patrick Deneen, the way to free society from liberalism is by forming smaller, faith and family based communities. What are your thoughts on Deneen's idea of a better society?

~~~

question 14

In one section of Why Liberalism Failed, Deneen talked about how supporters of liberalism never wanted to get rid of the aristocracy. Instead, they only wanted to replace it with a newer one that they saw as better. What is your opinion on this idea?

~~~

question 15

Patrick Deneen believes that society spends too much time focusing on small issues like corporations and the government's control. What is your opinion on this?

~~~

~~~

question 16

One reader suggested that everyone, especially people who belong to an organized, Christian religion, should read Why Liberalism Failed. Who would you recommend this book to?

~~~

~~~

question 17

In a review written by one reader of Why Liberalism Failed, the reader took issue in the fact the Patrick Deneen believes that liberalism has defeated fascism. What is your opinion on this?

~~~

~~~

question 18

One reader felt that Patrick Deneen never factually explained why liberalism failed. What is your opinion?

~~~

~~~

question 19

In the opinion of one reader, Patrick Deneen is "weirdly fixated" on gay marriage laws and sexual morality. What is your opinion on this topic?

~~~

~~~

question 20

Why Liberalism Failed seems as if it was written for those who already agree with Patrick Deneen's position, is the opinion of one reader. What do you think Patrick Deneen's goal was in writing Why Liberalism Failed?

~~~

Introducing the Author

PATRICK DENEEN STUDIED ENGLISH literature at Rutgers University, and has earned a bachelor of arts degree in the subject. He graduated summa cum laude and gave the commencement speech at his graduation from Rutgers. Deneen then went on to study Political Science at Rutgers University, where he earned a Ph.D. His dissertation for his Ph.D. Degree was The Odyssey of Political Theory. He was mentored by Wilson Carey McWilliams while writing his dissertation. Upon publishing his dissertation, Deneen was given the Leo Straus Award for Best Dissertation in Political Theory. This award is given out by the American Political Science Association.

He then went on to be a professor. He first taught Political Science at Princeton University from 1997 to 2005. Then, he went to Georgetown University to teach Political Science until 2012. At Georgetown he was given the Markos and Eleni Tsakapoulos-Kounalakis Chair for Hellenic Studies. After leaving Georgetown, Deneen went to teach at Notre Dame, where he still currently teaches. At Notre Dame, he teaches Political Theory and Constitutional Studies. He currently holds the David A. Potenziani Memorial Chair in the field of Constitutional Studies.

In addition to teaching at Princeton, Georgetown, and Notre Dame, Deneen has been a guest lecturer at several universities around the world. Some of these universities in the United States include Villanova University, Yale University, Eckerd College, Augustana College, Harvard University, Valparaiso University, the University of Pennsylvania, Hope College, Hillsdale College, Mercer University, and the University of Chicago, among others. Deneen has also given lectures at universities in Ireland, England, Germany, France, Poland, the Ukraine, Italy, Hungary, and Australia.

The first book that Patrick Deneen published was The Odyssey of Political Theory in 2000. Five years later, he published his second and third books,

Democratic Faith and Democracy's Literature. Deneen published was Redeeming Democracy in America in 2011. That same year, he also published The Democratic Soul. In 2016, Deneen published Conserving America? Thoughts on Present Discontents. His most recent book is Why Liberalism Failed, which was published in 2018.

Currently, Patrick Deneen has several book projects that he is working on. These projects include On Liberal Education: The Art of Being Free, Political Philosophy: A Short History, Liberalism and Conservatism: A Primer, and The End of Democracy: Tocqueville on the Fate and Destiny of America. Patrick Deneen is open to criticism on his ideas and his works. He has include links on his personal website to responses and controversies to his work.

In addition to books, Patrick Deneen has also written for several journals. Some of the journals he has written for include The Weekly Standard, The American Conservative, which he also edits for, and The Chronicle of Higher Education. He has also worked as an editor for Political Companions to Great American Authors and "Radical Conservatisms." He serves on the boards for American Political Thought and Perspectives on Political Science.

Patrick Deneen is married to his wife, Inge. They have three children together. Deneen and his family live in South Bend, Indiana.

Bonus Downloads
Get Free Books with __Any Purchase__ of Conversation Starters!

Every purchase comes with a FREE download!

*Add spice to any conversation
Never run out of things to say
Spend time with those you love*

Get it Now

or Click Here.

Scan Your Phone

Fireside Questions

"What would you do?"

Tip: These questions can be a fun exercise as it spurs creativity among the readers by allowing alternate scene endings and "if this was you" questions.

question 21

Patrick Deneen has studied Political Science and has earned a Ph.D. in the subject. Why do you think Deneen chose to be a professor of Political Science rather than do something in the government?

~~~

question 22

As a lecturer, Patrick Deneen has taught at many universities around the world. Why do you think so many schools want him to give lectures at their school?

~~~

~~~

question 23

On his personal website, Patrick Deneen has a section devoted to the responses and controversies on his work. Why do you think he is open to criticism on his work and displays it on his website?

~~~

~~~

question 24

Patrick Deneen's main focus in his writing is on democracy and liberalism. Why do you think he has an interest in these subjects?

~~~

~~~

question 25

To date, Patrick Deneen has published seven books. How likely is it that he will publish more?

~~~

~~~

question 26

Patrick Deneen writes that liberalism is failing people because it succeeded and "won" against fascism and communism. What do you think the world would look like today if fascism succeeded? What would it look like if communism succeeded?

~~~

~~~

question 27

One argument for the collapse of society due to liberalism is the advancement of technologies, such as cell phones, that make people more autonomous and more lonely. What would a world without cell phones look like?

~~~

~~~

question 28

An antidote to liberalism, according to Deneen, is building up a world that looks more like closer-knit, small communities based on faith and family. What do you think the positives and negatives of a society like this would be?

~~~

~~~

question 29

Patrick Deneen gives his opinion on what a better society would look like. If you could build a better society, what would your society look like?

~~~

~~~

question 30

Patrick Deneen's Why Liberalism Failed seems to be a book about where society went wrong and continues to go wrong today. If you were writing a book about what is wrong in society today, what key points would you add in to your book?

~~~

Quiz Questions

"Ready to Announce the Winners?"

Tip: Create a leaderboard and track scores to see who gets the most correct answers. Winners required. Prizes optional.

~~~

quiz question 1

Patrick Deneen argues that liberalism has failed because it has been _____. He uses the teachings of philosophers such as Sir Francis Bacon, John Locke, and John Stuart Mill to write his latest book, Why Liberalism Failed.

~~~

~~~

quiz question 2

According to Deneen, today's conservatives are actually _____ or "first-wave" liberals. Though, they don't realize it, today's conservatives and progressive liberals are actually helping each other move forward in their political goals.

~~~

~~~

quiz question 3

One of the problems that Deneen sees with society is the advancement of technology. He believes that the creation of _____ has made people more lonely.

~~~

~~~

quiz question 4

Another sign that civilization is about to collapse is the rise of the _____ culture. Deneen says that, even in schools, students are cheating more and becoming more rebellious.

~~~

~~~

quiz question 5

Deneen also discusses how liberalism has made way for a new form of _____. He explains that liberalism never intended to get rid of this political system, but rather, the intentions were to tear down the old system to create a newer version.

~~~

~~~

quiz question 6

True or False: According to Deneen, a society with smaller communities would be a better society than we have now. These societies would be based on faith and families.

~~~

quiz question 7

True or False: Deneen believes that it is a good thing that modern society has moved away from organized religions. He believes that organized religion has been the cause of many problems throughout history.

~~~

quiz question 8

Patrick Deneen studied English literature and Political Science at the same university. This university was _____.

~~~

~~~

quiz question 9

After completing his studies, Patrick Deneen went on to be a professor. His first teaching job was at _____ University. His second teaching job was at Georgetown University before taking his current position at Notre Dame University.

~~~

~~~

quiz question 10

True or False: Patrick Deneen also works as an editor. He has edited for "Radical Conservatisms" and The American Conservative, among others.

~~~

~~~

quiz question 11

True or False: In addition to being a faculty professor at a few universities in the United States, Patrick Deneen has also given lectures at several universities around the world. Some of the locations he has taught in outside of the United States are Italy, France, England, the Ukraine, and Australia, among others.

~~~

~~~

quiz question 12

True or False: The first book that Patrick Deneen published was The Odyssey of Political Theory in 2000. This was also his dissertation for his Ph.D.

~~~

Quiz Answers

1. Succeeded
2. Classic or classical
3. Cell phones
4. "Hook-up"
5. Aristocracy
6. True
7. False; Deneen sees the fading away of religion as a problem.
8. Rutgers University
9. Princeton
10. True
11. True
12. True

Ways to Continue Your Reading

EVERY month, our team runs through a wide selection of books to pick the best titles for readers and reading groups, and promotes these titles to our thousands of readers – sometimes with free downloads, sale dates, and additional brochures.

Click here to sign up for these benefits.

If you have not yet read the original work or would like to read it again, you can purchase the original book here.

Bonus Downloads
*Get Free Books with **Any Purchase** of* Conversation Starters!

Every purchase comes with a FREE download!

Add spice to any conversation
Never run out of things to say
Spend time with those you love

Get it Now

or Click Here.

Scan Your Phone

On the Next Page…

If you found this book helpful to your discussions and rate it a 4 or 5, please write us a review on the next page.

Any length would be fine but we'd appreciate hearing you more! We'd be very encouraged.

Till next time,

BookHabits

"*Loving Books is Actually a Habit*"